AF428187

"From Tears to Happiness: My Journey to Self-Love"

"A Story of Resilience, Friendship, and Discovery"

Author Name: Akanksha Matade

"Dedicated to those who have ever felt lost, alone, or uncertain. May my story inspire you to find your own path to happiness."

"Welcome to my story, a journey of self-discovery and growth. I share my experiences with vulnerability and honesty, hoping to inspire and support you on your own path. May you find comfort, guidance, and motivation within these pages."_

"From Tears to Happiness" "My Journey to Self-Love ."

"Dear Reader, This book is my
personal journey. "

"Happy are those who dare to carry
out their ideas and make their
dreams reality."

"As you embark on this extraordinary journey, remember that every step forward is a testament to your strength and resilience. May the pages of this book be filled with laughter, tears, and moments of profound growth. May you discover hidden facets of yourself, nurture your deepest desires, and emerge stronger, wiser, and more radiant. Embrace the unknown, for it holds the key to unlocking your full potential. You are the architect of your destiny, and every word, every thought, and every action is a brushstroke on the canvas of your life. As you navigate the twists and turns, remember to breathe deeply, trust yourself, and lean into the wisdom of your heart. May this journey be a sacred pilgrimage, a celebration of your uniqueness, and a testament to the transformative power of self-love. You are worthy, you are enough, and you are ready to unfold into the most magnificent version of yourself."

Before we dive into this enchanting world , I want to acknowledge the trust you've placed in me . Your time and attention are precious , and I promise to weave a narrative that touches your heart.

As you turn these pages , know that you're not just reading a story - you're becoming a part of my world.

Your presence is a reminder that words have the power to connect, inspire and heal .

"With every word , I'm unlocking my heart, freeing my soul , and sharing the whispers I've kept silent . This book is my symphony of secrets , emotions and life's melodies. "

A story of a young girl ...

"My story begins in a small village, surrounded by lush fields and rolling hills. It's a place where tradition and simplicity reign, where life moves at a gentle pace. But for me, this idyllic setting held a different reality. At just three years old, I was taken from the only home I knew and sent to live with relatives, leaving behind the loving arms of my parents.

Their decision, though difficult, was driven by a desire to provide me with opportunities they never had. As farmers, they knew the limitations of our village's education system and wanted more for me. They entrusted me to the care of relatives, hoping that the city's better schools would pave the way for a brighter future.

Little did I know, this journey would shape me in ways both beautiful and brutal. It would test my resilience, challenge my identity, and teach me the value of love, loss, and belonging.

In these pages, I invite you to join me on a journey of self-discovery, of growth, and of healing. It's a story of the human spirit's capacity to overcome adversity, to find light in darkness, and to transform pain into purpose."

About my family .....

"Growing up in a bustling joint family, I was surrounded by love, laughter, and a complex web of relationships. Our household was a vibrant tapestry woven from multiple generations, each thread intricately intertwined.

My family consisted of:

- My parents, loving and hardworking, who instilled in me the values of resilience and compassion.

- My younger brother, whose mischievous grin and curious nature brought endless joy.

- My uncle and aunt, whose guidance and support played a significant role in shaping my early years.

- Their two sons, one elder than me and other younger ,my cousins, with whom I shared countless adventures and formed unbreakable bonds.

- My grandparents, wise and kind, whose stories of the past sparked my imagination and fuelled my curiosity. Especially my grandpa .

Together, we lived under one roof, sharing meals, traditions, and memories. Our home was filled with the sounds of laughter, arguments, and endless chatter. It was a dynamic, chaotic, and loving environment that moulded me into the person I am today.

Little did I know, this seemingly idyllic setup concealed secrets, struggles, and challenges that would test our bonds and shape my destiny."

Mom and dad

My parents are the epitome of simplicity, love, and hard work. They come from a humble background, and their selfless dedication to our family's well-being is inspiring. As farmers, they toil tirelessly to provide for our needs, sacrificing their own comforts for our better future.

Their unwavering commitment to my education has always been a driving force in their lives. Despite the challenges they faced, they ensured that I received the best possible opportunities. Yet, in my youthful ignorance, I often misunderstood their actions and intentions.

Now, as I reflect on the past, I'm filled with regret for those misjudgements. I realize that their tough exterior hid a deep love and concern for my well-being. I wish I could turn back time and appreciate their efforts more.

To my dear parents, I want to say:

'I'm sorry for the misunderstandings, for the times I doubted you, and for not appreciating your love sooner. I love you both more than words can express. Thank you for being my rock, my guiding light, and my forever supporters.'"

"A CHILDHOOD OF SOLITUDE: MY JOURNEY AWAY FROM HOME."

"I was just a carefree little girl, lost in my own whimsical world, where laughter and imagination knew no bounds. The warm sun-kissed days blended together in a colorful tapestry of playtime, exploration, and innocence. But little did I know, my life was about to take a dramatic turn.

One fateful evening, as the stars began to twinkle in the night sky, my family gathered together, their faces etched with serious expressions. The air was thick with unspoken decisions, and I sensed a subtle shift in the atmosphere. Their hushed tones and exchanged glances hinted at a significant change on the horizon.

And then, it was settled. I would be leaving the only home I had ever known, bound for my relatives' house, where my educational journey would begin.

Everything was planned, and before I knew it, we arrived at my relatives' house. The unfamiliar surroundings and new faces made my heart flutter with a mix of emotions. As I stepped out of the vehicle, the crunch of gravel beneath my feet echoed through the silence.

My relatives welcomed me with warm smiles, but I couldn't shake off the feeling of uncertainty. Their house, though cozy and inviting, felt like a world away from the only home I had ever known.

As we settled in, I couldn't help but notice the differences. The layout, the furniture, the smells – everything was foreign. My relatives' voices, though kind, weren't the same soothing tones I was accustomed to.

That night, as I lay in the new bed, I felt a lump form in my throat. Homesickness crept in, and tears began to fall. I missed my parents, my room, and the comfort of familiarity.

But amidst the uncertainty, a spark within me began to ignite. A determination to adapt, to learn, and to grow in this new environment.

"A small kid wants nothing but the love of their mother and father's attention. The warmth of their embrace, the soothing sound of their voices, and the comforting presence that made everything right. But for me, those simple joys were torn away.

As I settled into my new life with my relatives, the ache of separation grew. Every passing day felt like an eternity without my parents' loving touch. I yearned for my mother's gentle kisses, my father's reassuring hugs, and the playful laughter we shared.

Their absence left a gaping hole in my heart, and I struggled to understand why I couldn't be with them. The questions swirled in my mind: 'Was I not good enough? Did I do something wrong?' The uncertainty gnawed at my innocence.

My relatives tried to fill the void with kindness and care, but it wasn't the same. Their love, though genuine, felt like a substitute for the real thing. I craved the unique bond that only my parents could provide.

As the days turned into weeks, and the weeks into months, I began to hide my tears. I learned to put on a brave face, to suppress the longing that threatened to overwhelm me. But deep down, the little girl within me continued to whisper: 'Mama, Papa, come back to me.'

"If a child lives away from their parents from an early age, they get disconnected – not just physically, but emotionally, too. The bond that once felt unbreakable begins to fray, like threads pulled from a delicate fabric.

As I grew older, the distance between my parents and me expanded, creating a chasm that seemed impossible to bridge. I felt like a branch torn from its tree, struggling to find roots in unfamiliar soil.

Simple moments, like bedtime stories, lazy Sundays, and family dinners, became distant memories. The everyday conversations, laughter, and inside jokes that forge a family's identity were replaced with awkward silences and forced small talk during occasional visits.

My parents' voices, once the most familiar sounds in my world, became echoes of a distant past. Their guidance, once instinctive and reassuring, was now fragmented and infrequent.

I began to feel like a guest in my own life, observing from afar as my parents' faces blurred into fuzzy memories. The pain of separation numbed, replaced by a dull ache of disconnection.

"Lost Childhood: A Tale of Longing and Resilience"

"I am not alone in my story. There are countless others who, like me, missed out on the simple joys of childhood with their parents. Our experiences may vary, but the ache of longing and the resilience born from it are universal.

We are the children who grew up too soon, our laughter and tears echoing through empty halls. Our parents' absence, though understandable, left an unfillable void. We adapted, survived, and thrived, but the scars of separation remain.

As I reflect on my journey, I see the faces of those who understand:

The child who moved away from home too soon.

The one who waited for parents to return from distant lands.

The youngster who endured the silence of divorce or separation.

We share a bond, a silent understanding that transcends words. Our stories may differ, but the emotions are the same:

Longing for bedtime stories and goodnight kisses.

Yearning for family dinners and lazy Sundays.

Craving guidance, comfort, and unconditional love.

Yet, amidst the pain, we discovered strength:

Resilience born from adversity.

Resourcefulness in the face of uncertainty.

Determination to create a better tomorrow.

If you, like me, have missed out on childhood's simple pleasures, know you are not alone. Your story is valid, your emotions genuine.

Growing up, I knew what it meant to feel alone, living far from my parents, I navigated the challenges of childhood without the warmth and guidance of those I loved most .

But still, "As the days turned into weeks , the silence felt suffocating. I longed for my parents hugs and reassurance."

I struggled with making friends living apart from my parents taught me self reliance, and the importance of the human connection.

Though my childhood was marked by loneliness, it shaped me into the person I am today . I 've learned to cherish relationships, appreciate the little things and find strength in vulnerability.

I'm sharing my story to let others know they are not alone in their struggles and may offer comfort...

"A Weathered Hand, A Gentle Soul"

Your hands, once strong and full of life,

Now wrinkled, worn, and creased with strife,

But still, they hold a gentle touch,

A comforting grasp, a loving clutch.

Your eyes, a window to the past,

Reflecting memories that forever last,

A twinkle in their cloudy haze,

A love that shines, come what may.

Your heart, a treasure chest of gold,

A storehouse of stories untold,

Of laughter, tears, and countless nights,

A legacy that shines with guiding lights.

With every step, with every fall,

You helped me up, through it all,

Your guidance, wisdom, and loving care,

A constant presence, always there.

Your love, a garden that blooms and grows,

Nourishing my soul, as the years unfold,

A bond that strengthens, come what may,

A grandfather's love, forever in play.

In your footsteps, I strive to stand,

To follow your path, hand in hand,

To honour your legacy, your name,

To make you proud, to earn your claim.

Grandpa, dear, your love remains,

A beacon in life's joys and pains,

A shining star that guides me through,

Forever in my heart, forever true.

THE LOVE OF MY GRANDPA:

When I was just 3-4 years old, living away from my family with some relatives, life felt overwhelming, but amidst the uncertainty, one person made my world brighter-*MY GRANDPA.*

As I sat alone in my relatives house , feeling like a tiny boat adrift that kept me grounded - my grandfather....living away from my family , I often felt isolated and unheard, but his periodic visits were the highlight of my month.

Grandpa would visit me every few weeks , and those 2-3 days were the highlight of the month. I'd eagerly await is arrival, watching the door for his familiar smile and twinkling eyes. He'd sweep me into his arms . Spinning me around in joyful circles, making me giggle uncontrollably. For those few days , I was the centre of his universe.

At night, we'd snuggle up together, and Grandpa would tell fantastical stories of brave heroes, magical creatures and far off lands. His deep voice would soothe my fears, and I'd drift off to sleep feeling safe and loved..

Grandpa was more than just a grandparent ;he was my confidant, my friend, and my guiding light . My fears , my dreams and my secrets. He'd listen attentively, offering word of wisdom and reassurance. His unwavering trust and support made me feel seen and heard.

Even at early age , I sensed grandpa's unwavering trust and support. I'd confide in him about my tiny troubles, and he'd listen attentively. His guidance helped shape my understanding of the world.

I cherish the memories of our late night conversations , giggling over silly jokes , and sharing stories of his childhood adventures. He'd take me on imaginary journeys , spinning tales of brave heroes and mythical creatures vanished, replaced by a sense of belonging.

Grandpa taught me the value of unconditional love , trust , and open communication. He showed me that family isn't just about blood ties but about the connections we make . Through him ,

Relationships build on mutual respect and understanding..

He made everyday moments extraordinary. My rock my shelter. His legacy inspires me to spread love and kindness wherever I go......

"My grandfather was more than just a grandparent; he was a multifaceted figure who embodied the roles of mother, father, brother, and everything in between. Not only did he shower me with love and attention, but he also selflessly cared for all my siblings.

Grandpa took on the responsibilities of a parent, doing everything with unconditional love:

- Feeding us nutritious meals

- Taking us on exciting outings

- Playing with us until we collapsed in laughter

- Tucking us in at night, ensuring sweet dreams

- Surprising us with our favourite toys and chocolates

He was the rock that held our family together, providing a sense of stability and security.

Grandpa's unwavering dedication and love created a warm, nurturing environment where we thrived.

This was the best time of my life ....

"Life was cruising along smoothly, each year unfolding like a perfectly crafted puzzle. School, holidays, and laughter filled my days. I was blissfully unaware of the drastic turn life was about to take.

But, as fate would have it, a new chapter was about to unfold, one that would bring unimaginable pain and loneliness. The carefree days of childhood were slowly fading, and the harsh realities of life were looming on the horizon.

I was on the cusp of a journey that would test my resilience, shake my foundations, and forever alter the trajectory of my life.

"My world was about to shatter, plunging me into darkness and despair."

"The only love of my life, my grandfather... His presence was my sanctuary, my safe haven. I had not imagined living without him, for he was the only person who truly understood me, who loved me unconditionally.

Grandfather's eyes sparkled like the stars on a clear night, reflecting a love so pure, so strong. His words, laced with wisdom and kindness, soothed my soul. In his presence, I felt seen, heard, and cherished.

Without him, the world seemed duller, quieter. Every step felt heavier, every smile forced. I wandered through days, searching for a glimpse of his warmth, his guidance.

But even in his absence, Grandfather's love remained. It lingered in the stories he told, the lessons he taught, and the memories we created together. His legacy lived on within me, a flame that flickered but never extinguished.

In the darkness, I held onto his words: 'You are loved, you are strong, you are enough.' His voice whispered in my heart, urging me forward, reminding me that I carried his love with me always.

"THE SILENCE OF LOSS."

I was seven years old, in second grade , when my world shattered. Life had been simple : school studies , and Grandpa's occasionally visits. But one fateful night , everything changed.

The phone call came like a thief , stealing away our peace .I was asleep, by the sudden rush of footsteps and panicked voices woke me . Aunt's trembling voice, uncle's rushed steps and the sound of car keys jingling- it was chaos .

"Get dressed, we have to go ." Aunt's words were laced with urgency.

I sat in car ,confused and frightened, as we sped through the darkness. The city lights blurred together like tears on a window pane. My heart raced with every passing mile.

At my house , chaos reigned . Family members hurried past ,tears streaming down their faces. Aunties wailed, uncles consoled and my parents ushered my siblings and me into a room .

" Stay here, kids. We'll be back soon."

Dad's voice cracked.

But I sensed it , something was terribly wrong.

My mother's trembling hand's lead us to grandpa's side . He lay still , surrounded by loved ones pleading with him to return. I stood frozen disbelieving. This couldn't be real. Grandpa, my rock ,my confidant, my everything.

Tears welled up, but I couldn't cry. My voice was stuck in my throat. I just stored, willing him to woke up, to hug me , to love me one more time .
But it was too late.

Someone whispered, "He's gone. " The words echoed like a death knell.

The room spun, and I felt like I was drowning. Mom pulled me close , buy I pushed her away. I couldn't process this.

The rituals began , a blur of tears and traditions. Fifteen days passed in haze, family surrounding us , then departing . Normally returned, but I was lost........

School resumed, but I felt alone . No friends to turn to , no words to express my grief . My shyness suffocated me

Grandpa's absence gnawed at my heart . I missed our laughter, our stories, our silence,. The world seemed empty without him .

I'd stare at the door , expecting him to come , smile and say , " Hey , kiddo!" But it remained vacant.

That night, I learned that life can change in an instant. The silence that followed was deafening, but it taught me to cherish memories and find strength in vulnerability.

He was my first love and his absence my first heart break.

Though life took me far from him, his love remains etched in my heart . Even today , when I close my eyes , I feel his warm embrace and hear his gentle whispers, he may not be physically present , but his legacy lives on.

"Echoes of Memories"

In silence, I hear your voice,

A whispered guidance, a gentle choice.

Though you're gone, your love remains,

A longing in my heart, a persistent pain.

At too young an age, I said goodbye,

Left with questions, a lonely sigh.

Your stories unfinished, your laughter rare,

A void within me, beyond repair.

Summer afternoons, once filled with glee,

Now find me solitary, lost in memory.

Your workshop quiet, your tools still,

A reminder of the hands that skilled.

Autumn leaves fall, like tears from above,

Reminding me of our last, precious love.

Winter's chill, a loneliness so deep,

A longing to hear your voice, to keep.

In this emptiness, I search for peace,

A sense of you, a heartfelt release.

Though you're not here, your legacy stays,

A love that guides me through life's maze.

In dreams, I see your smiling face,

A fleeting moment, a warm, safe space.

But dawn awakens, and I'm alone,

Left to navigate life's unknown.

 Your absence weighs,

A loneliness that time won't erase.

Yet, in my heart, your love will stay,

A beacon lighting life's uncertain way.

"TRAPPED IN SILENCE ."

"After his death, I felt like nothing was left. The anchor that had held me fast, the safe haven where I could be myself, was gone. I felt like going home, but now there was no place like home for me.

Every familiar corner, every cherished memory, seemed tainted with sorrow. The silence was deafening, a constant reminder of his absence. His chair, once warm with his presence, stood empty.

I wandered, lost and alone, searching for a sense of belonging. But every step led me further away from the comfort and security I once knew.

In desperation, I clung to fragments of our past:

A faded photograph, creased and worn.

A handwritten letter, yellowed with age.

A whispered phrase, echoing in my mind.

These relics became my lifeline, connecting me to the love and warmth we shared.

As days blurred into weeks, and weeks into months, I began to realize:

Home wasn't just a physical place; it was the love and memories we created.

Home was the sense of belonging, the feeling of being understood.

"Grandpa's passing shattered my world, leaving an unfillable void. He was more than just a grandfather; my best friend, and my happiness personified. Losing him at such a tender age was devastating.

To make matters worse, I wasn't close to my parents. We barely spoke, and I felt disconnected from them. Grandpa was the bridge that filled the gap, listening to my thoughts, sharing laughter, and providing comfort.

His absence felt like a crippling silence. I had no one to share my deepest fears, joys, and dreams with. The pain of losing Grandpa was exacerbated by the emotional distance between me and my parents.

   I was:

- Feeling isolated and alone

- Struggling to cope with emotions

- Lack of communication with parents

- Loss of sense of security and stability.

Grandpa's death taught me that life is fragile and unpredictable. I realized that relationships are precious and fleeting. His absence forced me to confront my emotions and seek new connections.

Life after heart break was a blur, everyone moved on ,but I remained lost. My parents, seeking better education ,sent me and my brother to live with our grandma in the city .

"My grandfather and grandmother were whole different personalities. Grandpa was loving, caring, and my rock, while Grandma... she was the villain for me. Her presence filled me with dread, her actions suffocating.

After Grandpa's passing, Grandma's grip on my life tightened. She seized control, dictating every move, every decision. My freedom, once a gift from Grandpa, was now a distant memory.

Grandma's rules were relentless, her criticism stinging. She monitored my every step, questioning my choices, and belittling my dreams. The warmth and laughter that once filled our home were replaced with cold, calculated control.

I felt trapped, caged by her restrictions. My voice, once heard and valued by Grandpa, was silenced. My opinions, dismissed. My feelings, ignored.

The pain of Grandpa's loss was compounded by Grandma's harshness. I felt orphaned, abandoned by the one person who should have comforted me.

But I refused to break. I found solace in memories of Grandpa, his words echoing in my mind:

'You are strong, you are brave, you are loved.'

I held onto those words, repeating them like a mantra, as I navigated the treacherous landscape of Grandma's rule.

"No playing outside. ""No meeting friends."" Focus on household chores. "

My brother enjoyed freedom while I was trapped. Studies suffered and tears flowed nightly , hidden from prying eyes.

Frequent illnesses became my escape. Father's concern took me to hospitals, and temporary reprieve to our village home brought comfort.

However, each return to Grandma was met with:

"You're faking it." "You don't want to study. "

Parents, relatives, friends and teachers doubted me . The constant taunts stung

One fateful day,

That day, the rain-soaked streets mirrored my turbulent emotions. My father's bike sputtered to a halt, and we took shelter under a nearby awning. His frustration boiled over, and his words cut deep:

"Stop doing dramas every time! We have work to do, and you're wasting our time and money on hospitals. If you don't want to stay, just come home and work in the fields. Stop this nonsense!"

His outburst felt like a slap. The pain and anger mingled with the rain, blurring my vision. I felt like I was a burden, a weight holding him back.

In that moment, I realized:

My father's love was conditional, tied to his expectations.

I wasn't allowed to be vulnerable, to be ill, or to need help.

My dreams and aspirations were mere "nonsense" to him.

The rain continued to pour down, but my heart felt dry, barren. I wondered:

Was this what life had in store for me?

Was I doomed to suffocate under the weight of others' expectations?

After that day, I erected walls around my health, hiding my struggles from my parents. The pain, the fatigue, the fears - all silenced.

In school, incidents piled up: fainting spells, lost consciousness, and unexplained ailments. Yet, I suffered in silence.

Teachers and friends noticed, but I brushed off their concerns. My parents' reaction to my vulnerability had taught me to conceal, to endure.

This secrecy became my shield, my survival mechanism. But with each passing day, the weight of unspoken words grew heavier.

I felt isolated, alone in my struggles. The fear of being judged, rejected, or burdened others with my problems kept me quiet.

My health suffered, but my determination to hide the truth grew stronger.

 That was the last time I fled to village for being sick . I adapted, becoming a silent, shy kid:

Attend school ,Return home ,Study ,No friends .

Longing for grandpa's love and protection, I'd cry in secret:

"Why did you leave me ?" "If only you were here....."

The ache persisted ,a constant reminder. Years passed ,but the scars remain . I learned to mask pain with silence, hiding true feelings beneath a stoic exterior.

My brother's freedom contrasted sharply with my confinement.

He'd:

- come home late ,sharing laughter filled stories.

- Attend birthday parties and social gatherings.

- Embark on trips with friends.

 I ,on the other hand, was :

- Forbidden from socializing

- Restricted to household chores.

- Denied permission to join friends

A small friend group lived nearby, often gathering on our stairs. They'd discuss school, tuitions and friends. I longed to join them but,

- As Soon as I approached, they'd fall silent.

- Awkward glances and exclusion followed.

- Even my brother participated in this silence.

 Their teasing stung:

" You're so boring. " " you never have fun."

Aunt's living nearby would mock me:

" come work at our house too." "You're so obedient, always quiet. "

Their jobs hurt , but I remained silent, fearing repercussions

Their actions made me feel:

Invisible , Insignificant , Unheard ,

Grandpa's felt deeper. I missed his protective love and guidance.

One day , I realized : Their behaviour was not my fault. I deserved respect and friendship

A spark of courage.

I began to:

Stand up for myself silently set boundaries with my brother. Avoid engaging with mocking Aunt's.

Small step , but: I reclaimed my voice inwardly asserted my presence.

" longing for parental love. "

As I watched kids enjoying with their parents, a deep ache grew within me

They'd:

- laugh together

- Go on outings

- share meals Mothers would lovingly prepare their children's favourite dishes for lunchboxes. I missed Grandpa terribly, but now I yearned for my parents love .

" Why can't I have that ?" I'd wonder " Why did they send me away?"

Doubts crept in : " Do they love me?" " Do they want me ?"

Comparing myself to others, I fell :

" Invisible " , " unloved" , " unwanted "

Every child lived with their parents, enjoying family life. I felt like an out cast .

"Why me ?"" is it because I'm not worthy of love ?"

Misunderstanding my parents decision, I believed:

" They don't love me ."" They abandoned me ."

Resentment grow : " Why did they send me to Grandma? " " Why can't I live with them?"

The pain intensified : " No one want me ." I'm a burden ."

Self doubt consumed me :

" what's wrong with me? "" Why can't I be loved like others?"

Hidden tears . Night-time brought tears, hidden under my blanket .

" God, why can't I have a normal family? "

" Why can't my parents love me ?" Longing for parental love and acceptance , I felt lost .

THE FORGOTTEN BIRTHDAYS

Birthdays, a painful reminder.

No surprise parties, No excited wishes, No loving visits ,

My family absence stung .

One year, everyone even forgot . No calls , no messages.

The saddest day of the year. I'd wonder :

" Am I worthy of love ?" " Am I forgotten? "Tears fell, hidden from prying eyes. A lump formed in my throat.

Birthdays, a time for joy and celebration, were merely a distant dream for me. In childhood, I longed for laughter, love, and attention on my special day. But my parents' absence made it a painful reminder of their neglect.

After being sent to my relatives' home, I doubted whether my parents had ever celebrated my birthdays. No photos, no memories, just an aching void.

I asked them about it, seeking answers:

"Did you celebrate my first birthday?"

Their response, a dismissive shrug:

"The camera wasn't working that day."

A feeble excuse, a hollow lie.

Photos of my siblings' birthdays lined the walls, a stark contrast to my own forgotten celebrations.

Their absence spoke volumes:"You're not worth remembering."

"You're not special."

The pain lingered, a constant reminder of my insignificance.

But I refused to let it define me.

My birthdays became a testament to resilience.

A celebration of survival.A promise to myself:

"You are loved."

_____A HOLLOW CELEBRATION _____

Their is a small ritual in Indian culture Grandma used to do it on my birthdays as,

" A token of love" , she'd say .

But it felt empty. No warmth. No excitement.

Just a obligation. I'd force a smile." Thank you !" But inside , I'd cry:" Why doesn't anyone care?" " Why am I so unimportant ? "

___LONGING FOR CONNECTION ___

I'd imagine:

A big part with friends and family, laughing and playing games . Feeling loved and cherished. But the reality crushed those dreams .

___ A SILENT SORROW ___

I'd hide my feelings. No one understood. Not even my brother. He'd enjoy his birthdays .I'd pretend mine didn't exist.

___ A PAINFUL PATTERN ___

Years passed, and the pain persisted. Birthdays became a dreaded day . A reminder of my insignificance.

Would anyone notice if I disappeared?

___ A NEW RESOLVE ___

Tired of sadness , I decided to change . Started making friends , started talking to everyone.

A friend circle formed . School became a refuse. Laughter and camaraderie filled my days

But nights remained tough. Tears fell, hidden from prying eyes . Longing for something more .

Hidden pain .

Incidents kept hurting me :

I used to sit outside house alone and just think about everything, but.,

Grandma's scolding: "you're watching boys !"

(me being just a 13,lost in thoughts)

When I visit to my nearby friends house that also very rarely, she used to complaint that - "I'm just wasting my time going with friends chilling outside and so on ." Then scolding from everyone. You should be responsible child as you are not staying with your parents. Show some maturity, Help your grandma with household chores, she is old now , even after doing everything that I can do , everyone blamed me for no reason.

RESILIENCE

I'd cry for 1-2 days .Ask God, why me ?"Console myself, " Move on ."

Life wasn't perfect, but :

It was better. I learned to cherish small joys

Friendship , Laughter , School.

A Fragile Balance Between happiness and pain .

I walked a tight rope , falling , getting up.

Smiling, hiding tears . Growing strength

With each challenge : I adapted, I coped ,

Lessons learned:

Resilience . Self compassion .Hope

The Journey continues.....

A TURNING POINT

One day, exhausted from the emotional
Rollercoaster, I realized:

I couldn't change others. But I could change
myself. Self- Reflection.

I began Journaling:

" what hurts me ?"What makes me happy?
"Insights emerged : I carved love and acceptance.

I needed self - compassion.

Self - Acceptance.

I started embracing my imperfections,

"I'm worthy, despite flaws." "I'm enough ."

Affirmations become daily mantras :

" I love myself. "" I accept myself. "

With newfound Self- awareness:

I set boundaries with Grandma . I communicated openly with friends.

Relationships transformed:

Less drama .More understanding , Forgiveness.

I learned to forgive :

Grandma's harsh words, Friends thoughtless actions , Freedom from Resentment

Empowerment . Self- acceptance . sparked: Confidence . Resilience . Purpose.

I pursued passions:

Writing dairy , Helping others , being happy alone.

Inner peace .Nights were no longer tears filled .Reflections became.

Gratitude lists .Goals .Inspiration.

I emerged stronger : Self assured .Compassionate

Authentic.

"Despite living with Grandma , I was determined
to make the most of my school experience. I
eagerly looked forward to school picnics,
cherishing every opportunity to break free from
my daily routine.

Each picnic was a vibrant adventure, filled with
laughter, games, and camaraderie. I revelled in the
freedom to explore new places, make memories
with friends, and simply be a carefree child

*A DAY TO REMEMBER *

I still vividly remember the day our class teacher announced, " school picnic!" The excitement was palpable , and I couldn't contain my joy . Seventh class was a turning point for mw , and this trip marked the beginning of happier times. After struggling with emotional turmoil and feeling lost , I finally felt like I belonged . Our teacher's words sparked a sense of anticipation, and I couldn't wait to share this experience with my friends.

I rushed home, eager to share the news with everyone . I called my father, asking for permission to join the trip. And he said yes .....

I felt was so happy . For once, I wasn't worried about Grandma's disapproval . This was my moment.

The day of the picnic arrived, and our class gathered at the bus . The atmosphere was electric laughter, singing and dancing filled the air. I had found a beautiful friends group, and we stuck together throughout the Journey.

Mostly me and one of the friend Robert (also not his real name).

Our destination was a water park, and the thrill of exploring it together heightened our excitement.

As we entered the park , screams of joy echoed through the grounds. We splashed water, went on rides, and gave each other dares to try the most terrifying attractions . Friends offered chocolates for mustering the courage to go on the roller-coaster. It was a day of uninhibited laughter, wet hugs, and sun kissed smiles .

For the first time in a long time , I felt truly carefree.

Time flew, and as the sun began to set , we reluctantly left the park. Tired but exhilarated, we returned to school, our hearts still buzzing from the adventure. The trip became the talk of the school , with everyone sharing stories and giggling over memories. We all agreed, it was the best day ever !

In the days that followed, anticipation grew. " when's the next trip?" We'd ask each other . The shared experience had bonded us , creating a sense of unity and belonging. For me , that day marked a turning point - I had found my tribe , and happiness was within reach.

Lasting impressions .

The school picnic's impact lingered . Friendships deepened .

Laughter echoed through corridors. Classroom discussions turned living . Teachers smiled , noticing our camaraderie...

Unfolding confidence.

I mixed with people, shedding inhibitions. Anchoring and conducting assembles.

Confidence soared .Everyone noticed.

Teachers admired me: " Bright student. "" Excellent work. " " outstanding performance. "

Scores improved. Exhibitions showcased my art .Finding my voice .

I expressed opinions. Participated in programs.

Public speaking lost its fear. Best year of my life .

Seventh grade became a transformative journey. From shy to confident.

Hidden talents emerged. Recognition fuelled growth.

Teacher's Appreciation .Their words echoed ,

Believe in yourself. You're capable. Unleash your potential. Fulfilment.

I felt seen ,I felt heard , I felt valued .....

"Friends: The Gems of My Life"

"Friends are the treasures I've accumulated over the years, and I'm blessed to have the best of the best. Among them is Robert, with whom I shared a special bond. We were classmates from the second grade, but our friendship blossomed in sixth and seventh grade.

 With other close friends, formed an beautiful group. They were the perfect blend of academic achievers, creative thinkers, and entertaining jokesters. We supported each other through thick and thin, sharing laughter and adventures.

Friends who were a dynamic mix of:

- Academic stars who inspired me to excel

- Creative minds who sparked imagination

- Entertaining friends who brought joy

- Helpful hands who lent support

Together, we navigated :

- Mischief and mayhem

- Punishments and laughter

- Memories that last a lifetime.

Unappreciated bonds

We took them for granted . Those laughter filled days . Those adventurous evenings , our school friendships .

We didn't realize their worth .

Only now remembering those days I understand the value of real friends, the importance of this carefree days , the strength of our unbreakable bonds . The memories we created....

BONDING WITH MY BROTHER

Years of living together, apart from our family, forged an unbreakable bond between my elder brother (cousin) and me . We had grown accustomed to relying on each other, sharing every aspect of our lives.

"Sharing laughter and secrets."

We began sharing stories about school, friendship, and crushes laughter filled our rooms as we reminisced about the adventures.

Small fights , Big lessons.

Despite our closeness , we weren't immune to disagreements." you always hog the TV remote!"

I'd exclaim.

" No , you always change the channel without asking!" My brother would retort.

Navigating Relationships

As we grew older, our conversations shifted to Relationships. " I have crush on someone ."

He confide : " who is she ? Tell me everything!"

Even I shared about boys, friends, crushes everything...

He offered guidance and support helping me navigate the complexities .The unbreakable bonds

From here , our connection solidified , A lifelong friendship formed.

"Growing up, my elder brother was the academic benchmark. He consistently outperformed me, scoring higher marks and earning praise from our parents. While I was no slouch, his achievements cast a shadow over mine.

Our parents, though well-intentioned, fuelled the comparison. 'Why can't you be more like your brother?' they'd say, their words piercing my self-esteem.

Despite this, my love and admiration for my brother never wavered. I recognized that he, too, faced pressures and expectations. We were both navigating the same challenging landscape.

I longed to see him happy and successful, and his accomplishments brought me genuine joy. Our bond transcended academic rivalries, forged in shared experiences and mutual rivalries .

Looking back, I realize that years transformed us . From siblings to best friends, our bond remains unshakable.

To my dearest brother,

Thank you for being my rock, my confidant and my guiding light . Your unwavering support and love mean everything to me .

For protecting me from harm's way , For keeping my secrets safe , For not being that toxic big brother , For letting me enjoy my own freedom, For not suffocating me with overprotection....

Thank you !

Thank you for the epic WWE matches after school, For laughing with me until our sides hurt , For believing in me when I doubted myself , For motivating me....

I'm grateful. For being my partner in crime , For sharing life's adventures together, For being my forever friend.....

Thank you but most importantly , I want to say

Sorry !

Sorry for misunderstanding you early..

Sorry for the times I doubted your intentions...
sorry for not seeing things from your perspective...

Your patience, understanding and love helped me
grow...

I love you !

. THE ROLLERCOASTER OF LIFE :

Life's unpredictable. Ups and downs, twists and turns . One moment , I was on tops .

The next , I plummeted

Summer holidays marked the shift . A carefree chapter closed...

A new , uncertain one began..

The End of a Era . Our friends circle shattered. Divided into different sections .

No more group discussions . No more laughter filled moments. No more friendships stories.

Separation Anxiety

I struggled to cope . Missing my friends. Longing for our gatherings . Our bonds , now fractured .

Drifting apart New classmates. New friendships formed .

But it wasn't the same . Those memories lingered .
Haunted me . Reminded me of what we lost . The
realization. Life moves on .People change .

Friendships evolve .But the pain remained .

A LESSON LEARNED

 Appreciate what you have , for it can vanish, in
an instant. Looking back, Those Summer holidays.
A turning point. A bitter sweet reminder , of life's
unpredictability.....

NEW BEGINNINGS

As I navigated the unfamiliar landscape, I stumbled upon a kindred spirit.

Fleeting connections .

Friendships , like life , are unpredictable.

Some people enter our lives . Teach us lessons . Leave us wiser , others fill our hearts , with love , laughter. But not all remain . Snakes in disguise. I encountered many. False Friendships . They sought help. Journals completed. Favour done . But when I needed. Them , they vanished.

The bittersweet truth

Not everyone deserves our kindness , our trust . Some snakes slither . Leaving scars . Yet , hope remained .

A Rare Gem . Among the crowd. One friend stood out . Genuine. Supportive .understanding.

Friendships , like flowers.

Some bloom . Some wither. But the ones that last nourish our souls .

Back to routine

School exams continued. Programs and events unfolded. Sports games heated up. Life moved forward .Time flew,

Before I knew it. School trip season arrived.

Excitement builds. Rumours spread . Destinations debated . Classmate buzzed . Anticipation grew.

Finally, the announcement . Our teacher revealed the trip location: scenic views, dam , parks. Adventure awaited .

Days passed slowly

Packing lists circulated , travel arrangements finalized. Count down began .

The Day Arrived. Buses loaded. Friends chattered . Excitement overflowed .

We departed .

Journey begins .winding roads , scenic landscapes , laughter and songs ... memories in the making .

As the bus wound its way excitement coursed through my veins. Two days of non stop laughter. Adventure and bonding awaited .

Reuniting with old friends. Sharing stories, that endless talks

THE JOURNEY BACK

Our last dinner together, laughter and memories.

Time to bid farewell . The bus Ride home . Tired
exhausted, and happy. Classmates settled in .
Snores and gentle hum . Bus wheels spinning.

Sudden Jerk .

Suddenly, the bus screeched . A punctured tire ,
gasps and groans

Sleepy eyes opened. Confusion and concern .

" What happened? " someone asked ." Puncture , "
the driver replied. " In the middle of nowhere ?"

Driver's reassurance.

" Don't worry, kids . We'll get this fixed . Safe and
sound. "

Calm and cooperative. We waited patiently. Some
chatted others dozed . Repair work underway .

Unexpected delays, hours passed ,sun began to set , hunger pangs grew .

" will we make it home tonight ?" Someone asked .

Depends on the repair . And the spare of tire . " The driver answered.

Everyone came across a decision that we'll call up a new bus ..... New bus , New concerns . Relief washed over us .

A new bus arrived . Another driver , 2-3 staff members accompanied. Cramped spaces . Adjustments made , I seek refuge . Exhaustion consumed me . I sat beside our Teacher . First row , supposed safety . Eyes dropping. Suspicious encounter. But then , I sensed , uncomfortable gazes . A man's piercing stare . My unease grew . Ignoring him didn't help . His persistence unnerved. Bus halted . Food break . My anxiety simmered. Disturbed and shaken , confusion and hurt . Decision made that moment sealed it . My last school trip . No more risks. No more discomfort. Transfer to another bus . We switched buses again . My resolve hardened. No turning back .

That trip taught me: Not everyone will understand you . Self care and boundaries are crucial......

RETURN TO NORMALCY.

We finally reached home , exhausted but relieved.
School resumed it's routine, and I tried to erase
the memories of that trip from my mind . But
they lingered , haunting me like a shadow. I kept
the painful memories hidden . The weight of those
experiences felt too heavy to share .

Exams on the horizon.

Days passed quickly and exams loomed near .
Preparations intensified , and focus was essential ,
I immersed myself in studies , determined to excel

.

Pandemic strikes .

Then , suddenly, news spread like wildfire :
COVID-19 had arrived , and a lockdown was
declared. Schools shut down , and life halted .
The world outside seemed to freeze .

But fir me the pandemic was the time when I lived
with my family for so long after years .

A silver lining . For me , the pandemic was like a blessing in disguise.

Return to roots .

After years of living away , I returned home . To my family's loving embrace. To the comfort of our home. Reunion with parents .

I cherished every moment with money and dad .

Laughter, stories and memories.

A sense of belonging.

Closeness Rekindled. Years of distance melted away . Bonding over meals , TV shows late night conversations. Treasured time. Pandemic induced lockdown became.

A gift , not a curse .

Precious family time . Safety and security. Home , where love and care enveloped me . No worries about food, shelter. A sense of peace .

JOINT FAMILY JOYS

Four siblings, endless laughter . Fights and tears , quality time , unforgettable.

Also I have a younger brother. Younger ones comes with over attention , over loved over everything for everyone . But the love is still strong . I also used to fell left out sometimes, jealousy crept in .

The distance. Living away from home. Feeling disconnected. Missing out on moments . Parental love , a longing. I carved mom and dad's love , attention, affirmation. Felt deprived. While my brother received it all . Bittersweet emotions . Lockdown reunited us . Mixed feelings swirled . Gratitude and jealousy. Love and Resentment . Reconciling emotion. As I spent time with my family. Parental love isn't divided. Multiplied nor subtracted.

Everything was smooth like butter and suddenly a new chapter started....

THE TEENAGE ATTRACTION.....

During Lockdown's isolation I started talking to someone online . Quite witty .

My heart skipped beats . Unknowing infatuation. We talked for hours , shared laughter, dreams I opened up completely. Blinded by emotions.

My world revolved around him . Long waits , fleeting moments . Awaiting his messages. Counting minutes. Euphoric when he replied. Crushing disappointment .

As I reflected on that tumultuous period , I realized that my infatuation had blinded me to the reality of the situation . I had invested so much emotional energy into someone who barely reciprocated my feelings , and it left me drained and heart broken.

The long waits for a single conversation , the countless hours spent day dreaming about him , and the neglect of my own well being all seemed like a waste in hindsight . My friends warned but I convinced that my feelings were unique and special , but the harsh truth was that I had been just a passing distraction for him , a way to alleviate boredom during lockdown. The pain of that realization was crushing, and I couldn't help but wonder what I had gained from that experience , aside from a deep sense of regret and a resolve to be more discerning with my emotions in the future .

The sudden departure left me reeling , plummeting me into an abyss of despair . Every waking moment felt like an eternity , and sleep offered no respite from the anguish . My mind raced with questions, each one piercing my heart like a dagger . Why did he leave? Was I worthless? Unlovable? Forgotten? The uncertainty consumed me , fuelling a crippling sense of self doubt.

I began to question my own existence , wondering if I was nothing more than a fleeting thought in his mind . Trust issues sprouted like weeds , choking out any remaining hope . Fear of attachment gripped me , and I built walls around my heart, determined to protect it from future pain . But those walls also tapped me , suffocating me with darkness .

The misconception of first love. Many romanticize it, elevating it to an untouchable pedestal. But I don't believe in its beauty. For me, it was a painful lesson, a stumble into naivety.

My first love was stupidity, a tangled web of emotions, miscommunication, and unrealistic expectations. I was the problem, lost in my own world, unsure of what love meant.

It failed, spectacularly.

But in failure, I found liberation.

I realized:

First love isn't always true love.

It's often a learning curve, a stepping stone.

A chance to discover oneself.

To learn from mistakes.

To grow.

I see friends' relationships blossoming, first loves turning into lifelong partners. I rejoice for them, genuinely.

Yet, I'm grateful mine didn't work out.

If it had, I might have missed:

Self-discovery.

Independence.

Resilience.

The journey, though rocky, made me stronger.

Maybe I sought solace in that relationship because
I yearned for someone to:

Know me truly.

Listen to my soul.

Love me unconditionally.

It wasn't love; it was a quest to fill the emptiness
within.

A hunger to be seen, to be heard.But he wasn't the
one.

He couldn't fill the void.Nor could anyone else.

For the emptiness was within.

A reflection of my own unresolved wounds.

My unspoken words.My unhealed heart.

The relationship failed.

"If my parents had loved me enough, I wouldn't be tangled in this web of attachment and insecurity. Their love would have been my foundation, my shield against the world's hurts.

But the absence of their affection left me vulnerable.Seeking validation in all the wrong places.Clutching onto fleeting connections.

Desperate for a sense of belonging.

Their love would have taught me:Self-worth.Self-love.Self-acceptance.Instead, I struggled to find these truths.

In the arms of others, I sought solace.But it was a mirage, a temporary high.Leaving me emptier, more lost.Until I realized:I must learn to love myself.To fill the void with self-compassion.To break free from attachment's chains.

To find solace within..

Days passed ....

As the lockdown finally come to an end , a mix of emotions swirled within me - excitement, nervousness, and a hint of relief school was reopening , and I couldn't wait to reunite with my friends. Share stories of our lockdown experiences , and start anew .

Now I was not going to live with my grandma because of covid she was at village. But my father quickly came up with an alternative plan , suggesting to stay with my paternal aunt and uncle instead.

Their house was nearby my school , making it a safer and more convenient option . I nodded in agreement, albeit with some uncertainty. Little did I know , this change of plans would bring about a whole new set of experiences and memories...

Upon arrival , my aunt welcomed me with open arms , urging me to make myself at home . My uncle chuckled, promising fun times ahead .

As I settled into their routine , I discovered the joys of exploring their neighbourhood, sharing meals , and laughing together.

As the days turned into weeks , I found myself growing closer to them . Our conversations flowed effortlessly, covering everything.

I even helped aunt with cooking, learning secret recipes and techniques. Uncle regaled me with fascinating stories of his childhood, leaving me in stitches. My cousin became my crime partner.

Initial uncertainty gave way to a deep sense of belonging. I'd never experienced before . Every moment with them was infused with love and laughter, from family trips to the scenic destinations , where uncle would regate us with the stories of his childhood, to our memorable dinners , where aunt's delicious cooking and uncle's witty joys would leave us all in stitches. Our nights walks under the stars were especially magical . Uncle sharing life lessons and guidance, making me feel seen and heard . Even our long drives were filled with music , laughter, and inside jokes , with uncle offering words of wisdom and spoiling us rotten ...

As I navigated my life with aunt and uncle's family. I also found solace in my friendships. We bonded over late night chats , sharing secrets, laughter and support. I helped them with their homework and they appreciated my guidance . Our friendships deepened, built on trust and mutual understanding. We discussing life , love and everything in between , engaging in philosophical debates and heart to heart.

As I was in my 10 th grade that time . The pressure mounted , and my uncle and aunt's expectations intensified. They constantly reminded me to focus on my studies, emphasizing the importance of securing good grades .

At that time I was so close to some of mu male friends and No one in our house like it .

However , when uncle and aunt discovered our texts , their concern morphed into anger , and doubt crept in . " concentrate on exams . " , they urge , " No distraction. " Forced to rely solely on studying to cope with the stress . The misunderstanding deepened , and resentment grew . I couldn't comprehend why they didn't trust me , why they saw my friendships as a hindrance rather than a help . Their restrictions only fuelled my frustration, making me wonder if they truly understand me . My friends, sensing my distress , reached out through other means , but even those attempts were met with disapproval. The tension between uncle, aunt and me continued to simmer , casting a shadow over our once harmonious relationship. As the exams loomed closer. I struggled to balance the pressure of performing well with the emotional turmoil brewing within , little did I know, this was only the beginning of a pivotal chapter in my life , one that would test my resilience, shape my relationships and alter my prospective...

Scoldings hurt, but it's not just the words that cut deep – it's the source. When we live with our parents, their scoldings, though painful, are tempered by love and familiarity. We know they care, despite the temporary anger.

But when we live with someone else – relatives, guardians, or strangers – their scoldings pierce like a dagger.

Every word, every tone, every glance feels like a rejection.

Their criticism isn't softened by warmth or understanding.

It's a harsh reminder: you're not one of us.

You're not loved unconditionally.

You're a guest, a burden.

Their disapproval echoes through empty halls, haunting you.

You question your worth, your identity.

Am I deserving of love?

Or am I forever flawed?

The sting of their words lingers, festering.

A wound that never fully heals.

THE DARKEST CHAPTER OF MY LIFE

That sunny holiday morning marked the beginning of the darkest chapter of my life . As I stood drying my hairs , uncle's casual touch sent shivers down my spine . I brushed it off as an accident , but deep within a seed of doubt sprouted. Repeated incidents followed subtle yet disturbing . Whispers, touches , and uneasy glances made me question everything. Fear and anxiety gripped me , trapping me in confusion. I froze in silence , afraid to speak out , fearing consequences and doubting my own sanity . Isolated and helpless , I felt trapped in a never ending nightmare .

As I reflected on uncle's actions , my intuition grew louder , warning me of impending danger . His lingering touch , the way he looked at me , and the subtle Whispers sent shivers down my spine . I knew I wasn't overreacting, my instincts were screaming for attention.

Girls are often socialized to doubt themselves, to question their own perceptions , but I refused to ignore the red flags . Uncle's behaviour was no longer just unsettling, it was menacing , fear and anxiety wrapped around me like a suffocating blanket , making it hard to breathe , hard to think.

I felt trapped in a prison of silence , afraid to speak out , fearing consequences, judgment and rejection.

The weight of uncle's actions crushed me , making me question everything . Was I being too sensitive ? Was I misinterpreting his intentions ? But deep down , I knew better . Mu instincts were spot on , and I couldn't shake the feeling that uncle's actions were a precursor to something more sinister . I struggled to find the courage to break free from the silence . Who could I trust? Would anyone believe me ? The doubts swirled, but my intuitions remained steadfast , urging me to seek help , to find a way out .

That fateful night , I was engulfed in a deep slumber, oblivious to the horror that awaited me . Uncle crept into the room , his presence a sinister shadow that loomed over me . His lips touched mine , sending a Jolt of terror through my body as I stirred awake . Disoriented and frightened, I felt hos hands fumbling with my clothes, attempting to strip me of my dignity . Panic set in , and I sprang up , my heart racing like a runway train. Uncle's face , twisted in a grotesque grin , was the last thing I saw before he fled into the darkness , leaving me shattered.

The rest of the night was a blur of anguish and confusion. My mind reeled , struggling to process the Trauma that had just unfolded. " What happened? " I kept asking myself , but the answer was too terrifying to confront. I felt violated , vulnerable, and lost .

Tears streamed down my face as I hugged myself tightly , trying to erase the sensation of Uncle's touch . The silence was oppressive , punctuated only by the sound of my own ragged breathing. I couldn't shake the feeling of being trapped; of being at the mercy of a monster who wore the face of a loved one .

As the darkness outside gradually gave way to down , my thoughts turned to escape . I knew I couldn't bear the thought of facing uncle again .

But where could I go ? Who would believe me ? The fear of not being believed, of being ostracized, kept me paralyzed . And yet I knew I had to find the courage to break free , to shatter the silence that had protected Uncle's secrets for so long .

Desperation drove me to dial Robert's number, my fingers trembling as I shared the horrific truth . His voice , laced with concern and shock , offered a fleeting sense of validation. For the time . I felt heard , believed. But our youth and inexperience left us feeling helpless , with the exams just a month away , I couldn't escape to my home . Uncle's presence loomed over me , casting a dark shadow that seemed inescapable. Robert's words of encouragement offered temporary solace , but the reality of our situation weighed heavily on us . We were teens , Ill-equipped to tackle the complexity of abuse .

The weight of my secret bore down on me , exacerbated the distance between my parents and me . Growing up, I had always felt like a temporary guest in someone else's home , never truly belonging.

My parents decision to send me away as a child had left on unhealed wound , a nagging sense of abandoned that I couldn't shake . Now , as I grappled with Uncle's abuse , I felt even more isolated, unable to confide in the people who supposed to protect me . The thought of sharing my trauma with my parents whim I barely knew , felt daunting , impossible.

Resentment simmered within me , fuelled by the question that swirled in my mind . How could they entrust my care to others ? Didn't they wonder if I was safe ? Didn't they care ? The pain of their absence , of their perceived indifference, cut deep . I began to hate them for their failure to provide a safe haven . Why they felt me vulnerable to predators like Uncle ? The anger and hurt boiled over , making it hard for me to breathe.

As I struggled to come to terms with my past , I realized that my parents actions , though well intentioned , had inadvertently created an environment conductive to abuse . Their detachment had left me feeling disconnected, unsure of how to seek help or whom to trust . The shame and guilt I felt were compounded by the fear of being rejected or disbelieved . My relationship with my parents , already tenuous , began to fray further . I felt like a stronger in own family, lost and alone with No one to turn to .....

Days turned into weeks, and weeks into months. I made a conscious decision to ignore Uncle's antics, diverting my attention to my studies. The strategy worked, and I found solace in my books.

Before I knew it, the tenth board exams arrived. I took a deep breath, put aside my distractions, and focused on giving it my best shot. The results were decent, and I felt a sense of accomplishment.

Finally, I returned home, and for the first time in what felt like an eternity, I felt a sense of belonging. Home was supposed to be a sanctuary, and now it truly felt like one.

Though the scars of the past lingered, I was determined to move on. Disappointment still lingered towards my parents for their inability to protect me, but the joy of being back home overshadowed those feelings.

I began reconnecting with old friends, sharing stories of my experiences, and finding comfort in their understanding ears. The familiar surroundings and loving support of my family helped me slowly heal.

"One thing I regret is not sharing my secret with my parents, not telling them about the pain and betrayal I endured at the hands of that man. I should have confided in them, sought their support and protection. Together, we could have brought him to justice, made sure he faced consequences for his actions.

But fear, shame, and self-doubt silenced me.

Now, I realize:

Sharing my story is a form of healing.

Breaking the silence is a step toward justice.

Empowering others to speak up.

Through this shared experience, I hope to:

Find closure.

Help others find their voice.

Ensure no one suffers in silence.

To those who've endured similar pain:

You're not alone.

Your story matters.

Speak up, and know you'll be heard.

And to my parents:

I'm sorry I didn't confide in you .....

My parents ....

With time, forgiveness replaced resentment, and our bond strengthened. I realized that my parents, though imperfect, had always wanted the best for me.

As I settled back into my routine, I made a promise to myself: to create a brighter future, one where I would never feel trapped or helpless again.

Little did I know, this was just the beginning of my journey towards self-discovery, resilience, and happiness...

Exams were over, and the time had come to decide my future course. My heart yearned to pursue journalism, uncovering truths, and amplifying the voices of the unheard. I envisioned myself writing impactful articles, shedding light on social injustices, and inspiring change.

However, my father had other plans. He envisioned me in a white coat, stethoscope around my neck, saving lives as a doctor. His dreams for me were clear, and he wouldn't budge.

I tried reasoning with him, sharing my passion for journalism, but he wouldn't listen. The argument ended with him insisting I take science, preparing me for medical school.

Though my heart wasn't in it, I respected his decision and began preparing for medical entrance exams. But deep within, I knew I wouldn't abandon my dreams entirely.

I made a silent promise to myself: I would pursue journalism, no matter what. I'd find ways to balance both paths, proving to myself and my father that following one's passion doesn't mean compromising on responsibilities.

With determination, I dove into science textbooks while secretly nurturing my love for journalism. I wrote articles in my free time, maintained a blog,

My journey was about to become a delicate balancing act between fulfilling family expectations and chasing my dreams.

I settled into the hostel, thrilled to start this new chapter. The coaching institute was renowned, and I was determined to excel.

Making friends came naturally, and soon I found myself surrounded by like-minded individuals. We bonded over shared aspirations, laughter, and late-night conversations.

Robert and I became inseparable. We spent hours exploring the city, trying new foods, and sharing secrets. Our friendship deepened, and I found a confidant in him.

Hostel life was a whirlwind of excitement. We'd stay up late gossiping, watching movies, or playing pranks on each other. Robert became my partner in crime, and together we created unforgettable memories.

Despite the intensity of coaching, Robert and I made time for fun.

One evening, as we sat alone , Robert asked, "What drives your passion for journalism?"

I shared my story . Robert listened intently, his eyes sparkling with understanding.

"You're going to make a difference," he said, his words filling me with determination.

With Robert by my side, I knew I could conquer everything...

As the months passed, I struggled to keep up the facade. Juggling coaching, journalism, and hostel life took its toll. The initial excitement wore off, replaced by exhaustion and stress.

I felt like I was drowning in a sea of responsibilities. Coaching demands intensified, and journalism projects piled up. Robert's support was unwavering, but even he couldn't alleviate the crushing pressure.

One year into this balancing act, I hit a breaking point. I couldn't focus on anything; my mind was a jumbled mess. Sleepless nights, skipped meals, and constant anxiety became my norm.

I began questioning my decisions. Was pursuing journalism worth sacrificing my well-being? Should I abandon my dreams and focus solely on coaching?

Robert noticed my decline and sat me down for a heart-to-heart. "You can't keep running on empty," he said, concern etched on his face. "What's the point of achieving success if you lose yourself in the process?"

His words struck a chord. I realized I needed to reassess my priorities and find a sustainable balance.

I took a step back.....

I trudged back home, seeking solace in familiar surroundings. But the frustration lingered, boiling over one day as I struggled to study.

"I can't do this!" I exclaimed, tears welling up.

My parents' response shattered me.

"You're distracted!" they snapped. "You don't try hard enough! You always make excuses!"

Their words cut deep, and I felt devastated. The pain and anger simmered, eventually numbing me.

I withdrew from everyone, including Robert. Our daily conversations ceased, and our friendship began to fray.

Days blurred together in a haze of despair. I accomplishing nothing, feeling lost and alone.

The passion for journalism, once a burning fire, dwindled to embers.

Self-doubt and fear consumed me:

"What if I fail? What if I'm not good enough?"

As isolation became my comfort zone, I realized:

"I need to break free from this vicious cycle."

Nights became my darkest hours. Tears streamed down my face as regret consumed me. Every decision, every choice, seemed wrong

"Should I have listened to my parents?"

Self-doubt and shame haunted me.

Everyone around me seemed to turn against me. Friends, relatives, even some family members.

"You're wasting your potential."

"You're not good enough."

"You should've stuck with science."

Their words cut deep, and I began questioning my own worth.

The medical entrance exam results only fueled the fire. I failed, miserably.

The ridicule and mocking that followed was unbearable.

"How did you score so low?"

"What happened to the bright student?"

The shame and embarrassment suffocated me.

I felt like a failure, a disappointment to everyone, including myself.

One night, as tears soaked my pillow, I hit rock bottom.

"I need to reclaim my life."

"I need to silence the critics."

"I need to prove myself."

A spark within me ignited.

A START OF A BEAUTIFUL
JOURNEY

"Divine Intervention: Lord Krishna's Transformative Embrace"

Lord Krishna's presence in my life was a divine intervention, a gentle breeze that soothed my battered soul. When darkness enveloped me, and loneliness seemed suffocating, He emerged as a beacon of hope. I recall the countless nights spent pouring my heart out to Him, sharing tears, fears, and doubts. His listening ear and compassionate heart healed my deepest wounds, restoring faith and reviving hope. Krishna's guidance illuminated my path, teaching me valuable lessons in resilience, self-love, and detachment.

As I embarked on this spiritual journey, His presence transformed my world. From feelings of isolation, I discovered connection and community. Pain gave way to peace, and darkness dissipated under the radiance of His love. Krishna's teachings became my mantra, inspiring me to cultivate devotion, seek knowledge, and practice detachment. Bhakti Yoga, the path of loving devotion, became my solace, nurturing a deep sense of connection with the divine. Through His grace, I rediscovered strength within, and resilience bloomed. Self-love flourished, allowing me to welcome loving relationships and meaningful connections.

Lord Krishna reunited me with supportive souls – friends who cared, family who understood, and mentors who guided. His presence in my life reminded me that I was never alone, that love and compassion were always within reach. As I continue on this transformative journey, I find solace in Krishna's timeless wisdom: "When righteousness is lost, I will emerge." His promise echoes within me, reassuring me that no matter life's challenges, divine love and guidance are always available. In Lord Krishna's embracing presence, I have found my haven, my peace, and my purpose.

"There was a time when self-doubt consumed me. Every reflection led to despair:

'I've failed as a friend, neglecting those who cared.'

'I've failed as a daughter, disappointing my parents.'

'I've failed as a sister, lacking support and guidance.'

'I've failed as a student, falling short of expectations.'

Every accomplishment seemed tainted by shortcomings. Self-criticism became my inner voice:

'You're not good enough. 'You'll never succeed. 'You're a disappointment.'

But one day, something shifted.

I realized:

Perfection is unattainable.

Everyone faces struggles.

Failure is a stepping stone.

Growth happens in the darkness.

I began to reframe my thoughts:

'I've learned from my mistakes.'

'I've grown through challenges. 'I've shown resilience. 'I've made a difference in small ways.'

Self-compassion slowly replaced self-criticism.

I acknowledged my worth, beyond accomplishments.

"I sought happiness in external validation:

Friends' laughter

Family's approval

Social media's likes

But the void remained.

Until I discovered:

Happiness resides within.

I prioritized myself, and:

My world transformed.

Joy bloomed in solitude.

Confidence radiated from within.

Self-trust became my compass.

I learned to:

Embrace quirks

Celebrate strengths

Forgive weaknesses

In this inner sanctuary, happiness flourished.

No longer dependent on external validation,

I stood tall, unshaken.

I took a deep breath, embracing a new journey –
one of self-discovery and happiness.

For the first time, I put myself first.

Dropping a year to focus on personal growth was
liberating.

Moving away from home, I rediscovered myself.

I prioritized happiness, and life transformed.

Days filled with:

Reading books that nourished my soul

Laughing with friends who uplifted me

Studying with purpose, not pressure

Writing from the heart, unleashing creativity

Self-care became my mantra:

Meditation and mindfulness

Journaling and reflection

As I blossomed, relationships transformed:

Family understood my needs

Friends supported my journey

New connections inspired growth

This break from convention became:

A bridge to self-awareness

A path to emotional intelligence

A journey to inner peace

Now, I smile, knowing:

Happiness is a choice

Self-love is essential

Growth is lifelong .

Robert and I reached out , my rock, my confidant.

"Hey, I'm back," I said, my voice trembling.

"Where have you been?" Robert asked, concern etched in his tone.

"I needed time to rediscover myself," I replied.

Silence. Then, "I'm glad you're back. I've missed you."

Our conversation flowed effortlessly, like no time had passed.

Robert listened intently as I shared my journey.

"I'm proud of you," he said. "You're stronger than you think."

With Robert by my side, I felt unstoppable.

Together, we:

Explored new hobbies

Discussed life's complexities

Supported each other's dreams

Robert's unwavering presence reminded me:

True friends stay, no matter what

Support and love conquer adversity

Second chances are precious

Now, I realize:

Robert's friendship was a lifeline

Self-discovery was crucial

Happiness comes from within.

This year was a dream come true. Every aspect of my life was falling into place, and I couldn't help but feel grateful.

My birthday was approaching, and I was nervous. Past birthdays had been marred by tears and sadness, but this year felt different.

Robert, sensing my apprehension, planned a surprise party with our closest friends.

On the big day, I walked into a room filled with smiling faces, balloons, and a gigantic cake.

"Tears of joy replaced sadness" as I took in the love and support surrounding me.

Robert handed me a thoughtful gift, his eyes shining with warmth.

"You deserve happiness," he said, his voice filled with emotion.

We spent the day laughing, sharing memories, and making new ones.

This birthday was unforgettable, a testament to the power of true friendship.

Robert's presences in my life was the best gift, a reminder that:

True happiness comes from within.

Friendship is priceless.

Life's beauty lies in simplicity.

As I blew out the candles, I knew:

This year marked a new chapter.

Happiness was mine to claim.

Friendships like Robert's were treasures.

Here's a conclusion to your story:

I've finally found happiness.

Surrounded by beautiful people, I've discovered:

Life's beauty lies in simplicity.

True friendships are priceless.

Happiness comes from within.

Robert's unwavering support and friendship have been a cornerstone.

Together, we've shared laughter, tears, and growth.

My journey, though imperfect, has taught me:

Resilience in the face of adversity.

Self-love and acceptance.

The power of true connections.

Now, I wake up with a smile.

Grateful for:

Robert's friendship.

My supportive family.

Every lesson learned.

Life may not be perfect, but it's mine.

Filled with love, laughter, and purpose.

I'm finally home.

"As I look back, I realize that happiness was within me all along. I'm grateful for the journey, the friendships, and the growth. Robert's presence reminds me that life's beauty lies in simplicity. I'm finally home, surrounded by love and laughter. My story may not be perfect, but it's mine, and I'm proud of who I've become."

"I've finally found my tribe, my haven, my sense of belonging. My small but mighty circle of friends has transformed my life. Two incredible women, my soul sisters, have shattered the misconceptions I once held about female friendships. They embody empathy, kindness, and unwavering support, always there to lend a listening ear or a helping hand. Robert, my rock, consistently offers words of encouragement and wisdom, while my brother-like friend provides unwavering loyalty and humor. Together, they've created a safe space where I can be my authentic self, free from judgment or expectation. We share laughter, tears, and growth, our bonds strengthened by shared experiences and vulnerability. No drama, no toxicity, just genuine connections that uplift and inspire me. I've learned to prioritize these relationships, nurturing them with trust, open communication, and empathy. In return, they've helped me discover my worth, my resilience, and my capacity for love. My little world, once fragmented and uncertain, now feels whole and vibrant, filled with purpose and joy. I'm grateful for these beautiful souls who've chosen to walk alongside me, and I promise to cherish and support them every step of the way."

As I reflected on my childhood, I began to understand my parents' love in a new light. Despite the distance that grew between us, I realized they did love me, but their love was often obscured by the challenges of raising a family. As the firstborn, I unknowingly shouldered responsibilities, sacrificing for my younger siblings. However, this sacrifice allowed me to discover the depth of my parents' love, though it was expressed differently. I saw their care in the late-night worries, their struggles to provide, and their silent sacrifices. My heart, once filled with resentment, now overflowed with empathy and compassion. I began to see my parents as human beings, with their own struggles and triumphs, and not just as caregivers.

This newfound understanding brought forgiveness and healing. I chose to let go of past hurts and embrace our imperfect bond. I celebrated our unique relationship, acknowledging the love that existed despite flaws. Proudly, I declared my love for my parents, flaws and all, and appreciated their efforts. In this journey of self-discovery and healing, I gained a deeper understanding of family dynamics, unconditional love, and connection with my roots. Our relationship evolved, and I learned to navigate ongoing challenges with empathy and patience. Through this transformation, I discovered the beauty of forgiveness, the power of love, and the importance of family.

"I've come to realize that God's divine hand has guided me through life's twists and turns. Despite my mistakes, He has consistently provided a path to redemption, correcting me with love and compassion. Compared to others, I've been blessed with a better life, and this realization fills me with gratitude.

God's wisdom has helped me:

Recognize the value of second chances.

Learn from failures, transforming them into growth.

Find strength in vulnerability.

Through trials and tribulations, He has:

Refined my character.

Sharpened my intuition.

Deepened my empathy.

I've begun to see mistakes as opportunities:

To learn and grow.

To seek forgiveness and healing.

To discover new strengths.

God's love has been my anchor:

In darkest moments, His light shone brightest.

In uncertainty, His guidance provided clarity.

In weakness, His strength lifted me.

This understanding has:

Fostered humility.

Cultivated self-awareness.

Nurtured resilience.

I am grateful for:

God's unwavering presence.

His unrelenting love.

His transformative power.

"As I close this chapter of my life, I realize that these pages have become a testament to my journey of self-discovery, healing, and growth. This book, born from the depths of my heart, has been my confidant, my therapist, and my sanctuary. Through every word, every tear, and every triumph, I've poured my soul onto these pages.

This diary-turned-book has been my catharsis, my liberation, and my rebirth. It's a reflection of my inner world, where shadows met light, and darkness gave way to hope. I've shared my struggles, my fears, and my dreams, hoping that someone, somewhere, might find solace in knowing they're not alone.

As I release these words into the world, I know that I've found my voice, my purpose, and my peace. This book is more than just a story – it's a testament to resilience, to the human spirit's capacity to overcome, and to the transformative power of love and forgiveness.

To anyone who has walked alongside me on this journey, thank you for bearing witness to my truth. May these words inspire you to find your own voice, your own strength, and your own path to healing. And to myself, I say: you are seen, you are heard, and you are loved."

"You are not alone. Your story matters. Keep shining."

Acknowledgments

A Heartfelt Thank You

As I bring this journey to a close, I want to express my deepest gratitude to everyone who has supported me along the way.

To my dearest one , who have been my rock, my safe haven, and my guiding light – thank you for your unwavering love and encouragement. Thank you for the trust and for everything.

To my friends, who have listened, advised, and stood by me through life's ups and downs – thank you for being my pillars of strength.

To Lord Krishna, whose divine presence has transformed my life – thank you for your boundless love, guidance, and wisdom.

To my inner self, for courageously facing fears, embracing vulnerability, and emerging stronger – thank you for your resilience.

And to you, dear reader, for embracing my story, sharing my tears, and celebrating my triumphs – thank you for being a part of my journey.

This book would not have been possible without the love, support, and encouragement of each and every one of you.

Thank you for believing in me, for inspiring me, and for helping me find my voice.

May this book be a reminder that you are not alone, that your story matters, and that love and forgiveness can transform even the darkest of experiences.

With heartfelt gratitude,

AKANKSHA MATADE .

www.ingramcontent.com/pod-product-compliance
Lightning Source LLC
Chambersburg PA
CBHW040145110726
48005CB00018B/2656